DAD
JOKES

DAD JOKES

A Collection of Cringey Crack-Ups

Slade Wentworth

ZEITGEIST • NEW YORK

Published in the United States by Zeitgeist,
an imprint of Zeitgeist™, a division of
Penguin Random House LLC, New York.
penguinrandomhouse.com

Originally published as *Dad Jokes: A Collection
of Cringey Crack-Ups* (Zeitgeist, 2022).

Zeitgeist™ is a trademark of Penguin Random House LLC
ISBN: 9780593435847
Ebook ISBN: 9780593690413

Author photograph © by Daxson Wentworth
Book design by Aimee Fleck
Edited by Erin Nelson

Printed in the United States of America
1st Printing

First 2023 Edition

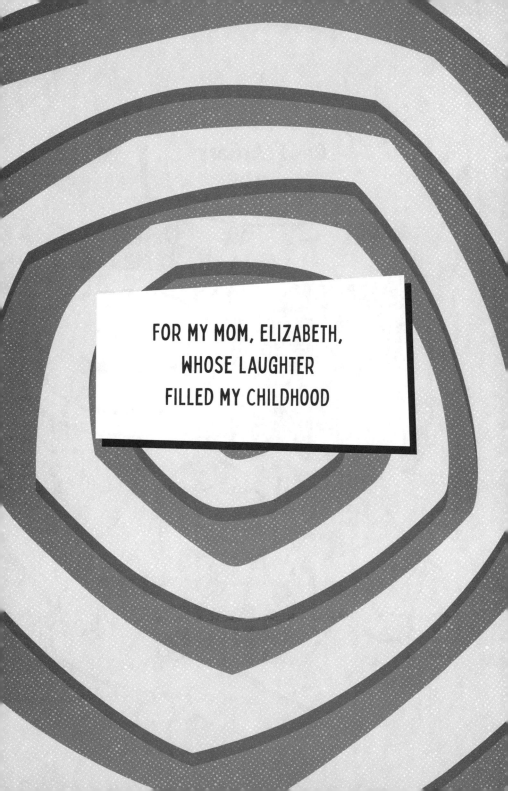

FOR MY MOM, ELIZABETH,
WHOSE LAUGHTER
FILLED MY CHILDHOOD

INTRODUCTION

What's a dad joke, anyway? Dad jokes are short and usually contain puns. Most importantly, they are *so bad*, they're *good*. In other words, they are the lifeblood of any comic's arsenal.

Whether you're holding this book because you pulled it off the shelf yourself or it was gifted to you from someone who appreciates your full-groan humor, you are in for a treat! This little book is jam-packed with dad jokes—enough terrible hilarity, cringey winces, and pun-tastic laughter to entertain all your family and friends.

Your assignment is to carry on the tradition and embrace your role as dad-joke teller. The people in your life need these jokes—in the car, at a backyard barbeque, in the office parking lot, or anywhere you can find an unsuspecting victim . . . um, that is, a grateful audience.

So, go boldly through these pages and get those knees slapped and sides split. I wish you an eye-rolling good time!

Some people like elevators;
some like escalators. Depends
on how they were raised.

. . . .

Q: What do you call two monkeys
who share an Amazon account?

A: Prime mates.

. . . .

I once got fired from a canned juice factory.
Apparently, I couldn't concentrate.

. . . .

Q: Did you hear about the gardener
who was so excited for spring?

A: Yep, they wet their plants.

I had a neck brace fitted years ago,
and I've never looked back since.

· · · · · · · · · · · ·

Q: What's brown and sticky?

A: A stick.

· · · · · · · · · · · ·

Sometimes when I have a moment to
relax, I spend time looking at my ceiling.
I'm not sure if it's the best ceiling in the
world, but it's definitely up there.

· · · · · · · · · · · ·

If a baby refuses to nap, is he
guilty of resisting a rest?

Q: What did one knife say to the other?

A: "Hey, lookin' sharp."

. . . .

Dear Math,
Please grow up and
solve your own problems.

. . . .

I can't find my *Gone in 60 Seconds*
DVD. It was here a minute ago.

. . . .

Today, my son asked, "Can I have a
bookmark?" and I burst into tears.
He's 11 years old, and he still doesn't
know my name is Brian.

Q: What kind of medical professional is Dr Pepper?

A: A fizzician.

. . . .

If sweet dreams are made of cheese, who am I to dis-a-brie?

. . . .

Q: What do you call a laughing jar of mayonnaise?

A: LMAYO.

. . . .

HER: I'm leaving. I am sick of you wearing a different T-shirt every half an hour.

ME: Wait. I can change.

Q: Which cat is the least loyal?

A: A cheetah.

. . . .

They say the sun is smart because it has about a million degrees.

. . . .

Q: Where did the hippie's wife live?

A: Mississippi.

. . . .

Lost my job at the bank on my first day. A customer asked me to check his balance, so I pushed him over.

Q: Did you hear about the weather
joke with a terrible punch line?

A: Very anti-climatic.

. . . .

I think I did well in my job interview
today. The supervisor said they were
looking for somebody responsible.
"Look no further," I said. "Whenever there
was trouble at my previous company,
they always said I was responsible!"

. . . .

Q: What happens when you
don't pay your exorcist?

A: You get repossessed.

Well, to be Frank with you, I'd
have to change my name.

. . . .

I had a fun childhood. My dad used
to push me down the hill in old tires.
Those were the Goodyears.

. . . .

Q: What do you say to your
sister when she's crying?

A: "Are you having a crisis?"

. . . .

I named my printer Bob Marley
because it's always jammin'.

Q: What's a computer's favorite snack?

A: Microchips!

. . . .

There was once a king who was only 12 inches tall. Say what you will, but he made a great ruler.

. . . .

I just found out I'm color-blind. The diagnosis came out of the green.

A group of chess enthusiasts checked in to a hotel and were standing in the lobby discussing their recent tournament victories. After about an hour, the manager came out of the office and asked them to disperse. "But why?" they asked. "Because," he said, "I can't stand chess nuts boasting in an open foyer."

. . . .

They say that 4/3 of people are bad at fractions.

. . . .

Q: Did you hear about the award given to the inventor of the knock-knock joke?

A: Yeah, the No Bell Prize.

I used to run a dating service for chickens, but I was struggling to make hens meet.

. . . .

Q: What did the two slices of bread say on their wedding day?

A: "It was loaf at first sight."

. . . .

The future, the present, and the past walk into a bar. Things got a little tense.

. . . .

As a lumberjack, I've cut down exactly 2,417 trees. I'm certain of this number, because every time I cut one down, I keep a log.

I installed a bar on my roof. Now I enjoy telling my guests that their drinks are on the house.

. . . .

Q: Can February march?

A: No, but April may.

. . . .

As I handed my aunt her 50th birthday card, she became emotional and said, "You know, one card would have been enough."

. . . .

Q: What did one hat say to the other?

A: "Stay here! I'm going on ahead."

A friend came to me for advice and asked whether she should have a baby after 40. I said that I didn't think so; 40 babies are probably enough.

. . . .

Q: What kind of tea is the hardest to swallow?

A: Reality.

. . . .

My friend was showing me his tool shed and pointed to a ladder. "That's my stepladder," he said, a little teary. "I never knew my real ladder."

My recliner and I go way back.

• • • • • • • • • • • •

Q: Why was the broom late for work?

A: It overswept.

• • • • • • • • • • •

A jumper cable walks into a bar.
The bartender says, "I'll serve you,
but don't start anything."

• • • • • • • • • • •

A soccer ball walks into a bar, and
the bartender kicks him out.

A guy walks into a bar. Disqualified
from the limbo contest.

. . . .

A magician walks down an
alley and turns into a bar.

. . . .

Two guys walked into a bar.
The third guy ducked.

. . . .

I was teaching my kids how to perform
addition using double digits. That was in tens.

Q: What do sprinters eat before a race?

A: Nothing. They fast!

· · · · · · · · · · ·

I was angry at my friend Mark for stealing my dictionary. I yelled at him, "Mark, my words!"

· · · · · · · · · · ·

Q: What is the tallest building in the world?

A: The library. It has the most stories.

· · · · · · · · · · ·

My partner demanded that I stop acting like a flamingo. So I had to put my foot down.

A guy goes to his doctor because he can see into the future. The doctor asks him, "How long have you suffered from this condition?" The guy tells her, "Since next Monday."

. . . .

Q: What did the pirate say
on his 80th birthday?

A: "Aye, Matey."

. . . .

There's a thin line between a numerator and a denominator. Only a fraction of people understand this.

I don't like to attend funerals that start before noon. I'm not a mourning person.

. . . .

Q: What do you call a wizard
who's really bad at football?
A: Fumbledore.

. . . .

At first, my dad didn't like the revolving
chair I bought him. But after sitting
in it for a while, he came around.

. . . .

Rest in peace, boiling water. You will be mist.

Q: Did you hear about the
rising cost of balloons?

A: Classic case of inflation.

. . . .

Don't you hate it when someone
answers their own question? I do.

. . . .

Q: What did the three-legged dog say
when he walked into a saloon?

A: "I'm looking for the man
who shot my paw."

. . . .

A slice of apple pie costs $2.50 in Jamaica.
In the Bahamas, it costs $3.00. These
are the pie rates of the Caribbean.

Q: How do you tell the difference between a bull and a cow?

A: It is either one or the udder.

. . . .

If money doesn't grow on trees, then why do banks have branches?

. . . .

When I was a kid, my mom told me I could be anyone I wanted. Turns out identity theft is a crime.

. . . .

Q: What sound does a witch's car make?

A: *Broom, broom.*

I went to buy a pair of camouflage pants, but I couldn't find any.

· · · · · · · · · · · ·

Q: Did you hear about the break-in at the parking garage?

A: It was wrong on so many levels.

· · · · · · · · · · · ·

Q: What's black and white and goes around and around?

A: A penguin in a revolving door.

· · · · · · · · · · · ·

I'm thinking about removing my spine. I feel like it's only holding me back.

Q: What lies at the bottom of
the ocean and twitches?

A: A nervous wreck.

. . . .

A man found a magic lamp with a genie
that offered him three wishes. The man
said, "For my first wish, I'd like to be
rich." "OK, Rich," said the genie. "What
would you like for your second wish?"

. . . .

They say money talks, but all
mine says is "Goodbye!"

. . . .

I was fired from my job at the calendar printer
just because I took a couple of days off.

Q: What did one wall say to the other?

A: "I'll meet you at the corner."

· · · · · · · · · · · ·

I have a joke about construction,
but I'm still working on it.

· · · · · · · · · · · ·

Q: Why couldn't the bicycle stand up by itself?

A: It was two tired.

· · · · · · · · · · · ·

Most people are shocked to find
out I'm a terrible electrician.

Q: Did you hear about the snowman
that threw a tantrum?

A: It was a real meltdown.

• • • • • • • • • • •

I used to think I was indecisive.
Now I'm not so sure.

• • • • • • • • • • •

I'm reading an antigravity book.
It's impossible to put down!

• • • • • • • • • • •

Q: How much room is needed
for fungi to grow?

A: As mushroom as possible.

I saw an advertisement in a store window that said, "Television for sale, $1.00, volume is stuck on max." I thought, "I can't turn that down."

. . . .

Q: What is the scariest tree?

A: Bamboo!

. . . .

I could tell a joke about pizza,
but it's a little cheesy.

. . . .

Q: When does a joke become a dad joke?

A: When it becomes apparent.

Q: What did the coffee report to the police?

A: A mugging.

. . . .

Q: Did I tell you about the time I fell in love during a backflip?

A: I was heels over head!

. . . .

Q: Why don't eggs tell jokes?

A: They'd crack each other up.

. . . .

The easiest time to add insult to injury is when you are signing someone's cast.

Q: Why do stand-up comedians perform poorly in Hawaii?

A: Because the audience only responds with a low ha.

. . . .

I'm thinking of having my ashes stored in a glass urn. Remains to be seen.

. . . .

I told my boss three companies were after me and I needed a raise to stay at my job. We haggled for a few minutes, and he gave me a 5 percent raise. As we were leaving his office, he stopped and asked me, "By the way, which companies were after you?" I responded, "The gas, electric, and cable companies."

My son got angry when I said, "The sky is the limit for you." Apparently he wants to be an astronaut.

. . . .

Q: What happens when it rains cats and dogs?

A: You have to be careful not to step in a poodle.

. . . .

ME: Bro, can you pass me that pamphlet?

MY FRIEND: Brochure.

. . . .

I was having difficulty fastening my seat belt, and then it just clicked.

Q: How does the moon cut his hair?

A: Eclipse it.

. . . .

People who use selfie sticks need to take a good, long look at themselves.

. . . .

DOCTOR: I think your DNA is backward.

ME: . . . AND?

. . . .

I just burned 2,000 calories. That's the last time I leave brownies in the oven while I nap.

Q: What do you call a magician
who loses his magic?

A: Ian.

. . . .

It takes a lot of balls to golf the way I do.

. . . .

DAD: I named you after my father.

AFTER MY FATHER: I know.

. . . .

Q: Why do plants hate math?

A: It gives them square roots.

Q: Why are ghosts such bad liars?

A: You can see right through them.

. . . .

Always borrow money from a pessimist.
They'll never expect it back.

. . . .

Q: How do caterpillars swim?

A: Using the butterfly stroke.

. . . .

SON: Dad, there is someone at
the door to collect donations for a
community swimming pool.

DAD: OK, give them a glass of water.

Q: What do you call an angry carrot?

A: A steamed veggie.

. . . .

The best gift I ever received was a broken drum. You can't beat it.

. . . .

Q: Why did the football coach go to the bank?

A: To get his quarter back.

. . . .

Q: What did the plumber say to the singer?

A: "Nice pipes."

I can't stress enough the importance
of developing a strong vocabulary. If I
had known the difference between the
words *antidote* and *anecdote*, one of
my best friends would still be alive.

. . . .

Q: Why did Snoop Dogg need an umbrella?

A: Fo' drizzle.

. . . .

Two sharks are eating a clown. One says to
the other, "Does this taste funny to you?"

. . . .

Q: What do you call a boomerang
that doesn't come back?

A: A stick.

The shovel was a groundbreaking invention.

· · · · · · · · · · ·

Today I found out that the local man killed by a falling piano will have a low-key funeral.

· · · · · · · · · · ·

Q: What's the difference between a poorly dressed man on a tricycle and a well-dressed man on a bicycle?

A: Attire.

· · · · · · · · · · ·

A cheese factory in France exploded.
Da brie is everywhere!

Q: Why was Pavlov's hair so soft?

A: He conditioned it.

. . . .

Q: Why do you never see elephants hiding in trees?

A: Because they're so good at it.

. . . .

My uncle named his dogs Rolex and Timex. They're his watch dogs.

. . . .

The grocery store clerk asked me if I wanted my milk in a bag. I had to tell him, "No, I'd prefer that it stays in the carton!"

An apple a day keeps the doctor
away. If you throw it hard enough.

. . . .

Q: Where do pirates get their hooks?

A: Secondhand stores.

. . . .

Q: Did you hear about the baby
who made a tissue dance?

A: He put a little boogie in it.

. . . .

A ship carrying red paint and a ship carrying
blue paint collided in the middle of the
ocean. Both crews were marooned.

Q: Which side of a tree grows
the most branches?

A: The outside.

. . . .

Q: Why are peppers the best at archery?

A: Because they habanero.

. . . .

I asked my son, "What's two minus
two?" He said nothing.

. . . .

Q: Why is Peter Pan always flying?

A: Because he Neverlands.

A famous art thief attempted to steal paintings from the Louvre in Paris, but he was caught two blocks away because his van ran out of gas. When the police found him, all he could say was, "I had no Monet to buy Degas and make the Van Gogh, so I decided to steal the paintings because I had nothing Toulouse."

. . . .

Q: Why was the calendar afraid?

A: Its days were numbered.

. . . .

I was going to tell a time-traveling joke, but you didn't like it.

. . . .

Q: What does a vegetarian zombie eat?

A: GRAAAIINS!

Two goldfish are in a tank. One says to the other, "Do you know how to drive this thing?"

．．．．．．．．．．．

Q: Where do dentists like to visit?

A: Floss Vegas.

．．．．．．．．．．．

Q: What did the janitor say when he popped out of the closet?

A: "Supplies!"

．．．．．．．．．．．

A rancher had 48 cows on his property, but when he rounded them up, he had 50.

Q: What did the grape do when
he got stepped on?

A: He let out a little wine.

. . . .

A man is washing his car with his son. The
son asks, "Can't you just use a sponge?"

. . . .

A man goes to the eye doctor, and
the receptionist asks why he's there.
He replies, "I've been seeing spots in
front of my eyes." The receptionist asks,
"Have you ever seen an ophthalmologist
before?" The man says, "No, just spots."

. . . .

Q: What does a baby computer call its father?

A: Data.

Before you criticize someone, walk a mile in their shoes. That way, you're a mile away and you have their shoes.

. . . .

I used to dislike facial hair, but then it started to grow on me.

. . . .

Q: Why did the kids take scissors to their joke book?

A: Dad told them to cut the comedy.

. . . .

Last night I dreamed I was a muffler. I woke up exhausted.

I was fed up with my wife's accusation that I have a poor sense of direction. So, I packed up my stuff and right.

· · · · · · · · · · ·

Q: Did you hear about the $0.45 concert?

A: It's 50 Cent featuring Nickelback.

· · · · · · · · · · ·

I don't trust those trees. They seem shady.

· · · · · · · · · · ·

I don't trust those stairs. They're up to something.

We all know about Murphy's Law: anything that can go wrong will go wrong. But have you ever heard of Cole's Law? It's thinly sliced cabbage.

. . . .

Q: How do light bulbs say good night?

A: "I love you watts and watts!"

. . . .

I used to play the piano by ear.
Now I use my hands.

. . . .

I have a joke about chemistry, but I don't think it will get a reaction.

Q: Why do dogs run in circles?

A: It's easier than running in triangles.

. . . .

Long fairy tales tend to dragon.

. . . .

Q: What is faster: hot or cold?

A: Hot. You can always catch a cold.

. . . .

I was just reminiscing about the beautiful herb garden I had growing up. Good thymes.

Q: Why is Saturday the strongest day?

A: That's when the weak ends.

.   .   .   .

I saw a baby owl caught in the
rain. It was a moist owlet.

.   .   .   .

Q: What do thesauruses prefer for breakfast?

A: Synonym rolls.

.   .   .   .

A steak pun is a rare medium done well.

Q: Did you hear about the raisin
that went out with the prune?

A: Couldn't find a date.

. . . .

A banker kept pestering me with all kinds of
offers. Finally, I told him to leave me a loan.

. . . .

Q: What do snowmen do in their spare time?

A: They just chill.

. . . .

Q: What does a skeleton say before dinner?

A: "Bone appétit."

I didn't think orthopedic shoes would help, but I stand corrected.

. . . .

Q: Why don't crabs give to charity?

A: They're a real shellfish breed.

. . . .

Q: What does a computerized frog say?

A: "Reboot, reboot, reboot . . ."

. . . .

I was shopping in a bookstore and couldn't find what I was looking for. The shopkeeper said, "Can I help you, sir?" "Sure," I responded. "Can you help me find a play by Shakespeare?" "Which one?" the shopkeeper asked. "Um," I answered, surprised he didn't know. "William."

I made a pencil with an eraser at both ends. It was pointless.

. . . .

Q: What superpower do you get when you become a parent?

A: Supervision.

. . . .

Q: Why do pirates have trouble singing the alphabet?

A: They get lost at C.

. . . .

A friend of mine went to mime school, and I never heard from him again.

Q: What's the best part about living in Switzerland?

A: I'm not sure, but the flag is a big plus.

. . . .

I decided to sell our vacuum cleaner. It was just gathering dust.

. . . .

Q: Have you heard about the restaurant on the moon?

A: Great food, no atmosphere.

. . . .

I didn't want to believe that my dad was stealing from his job as a road worker. But when I got home, all the signs were there.

Q: What does a clock do when it's hungry?

A: It goes back four seconds.

. . . .

I can't stand elevators. They
drive me up a wall.

. . . .

Last week my partner and I built an
igloo. Our friends came over and
threw us a housewarming party.
Now we're back to square one.

. . . .

I thought culinary school was
going to be difficult, but the final
exam was a piece of cake.

Q: Why do dogs float in water?

A: Because they are good buoys.

. . . .

My new neighbors haven't put
house numbers on their home yet.
They really should address that.

. . . .

My friend said he didn't understand what
cloning is. I said that makes two of us.

. . . .

Q: Why do seagulls fly over the sea?

A: If they flew over the bay,
they'd be called bagels.

Someone has been stealing the dogs in our neighborhood. The police say they have several leads.

. . . .

I finished my first week of excavation training. So far, I'm really digging it.

. . . .

Q: Did you hear about the couple who spent $1,000 on their front door?

A: Always making a grand entrance.

. . . .

I spent a lot of time, money, and effort kid-proofing the house . . . but the kids still get in.

Q: Did you hear about my neighbor who was 50 years old, delivers babies for a living, and just bought a new car?

A: Classic midwife crisis.

. . . .

Q: Why are snails bad at racing?

A: They can be sluggish.

. . . .

My partner caught me kicking ice cubes that had fallen on the kitchen floor underneath the refrigerator. At first, she was annoyed. Now it's water under the fridge.

. . . .

I wrote a joke about German sausages, but it was the wurst.

Q: Did you hear about the sandwich that couldn't stop telling jokes?

A: It was on a roll.

. . . .

Q: Why did the stadium get so hot after the game?

A: All of the fans left.

. . . .

They say the desserts in Italy are the best in the world. I've never been, so I cannoli imagine.

. . . .

Some people can't tell the difference between entomology and etymology. They bug me in ways I can't put into words.

I hate it when people say age is just
a number. Age is clearly a word.

• • • • • • • • • • •

Q: Why did the composer stay in bed?
A: To finish writing their sheet music.

• • • • • • • • • • •

A travel agent told me they could
get me a free trip to Egypt if I could
get five other people to sign up. It
sounded like a pyramid scheme.

• • • • • • • • • • •

Q: What state is known for its small drinks?
A: Minnesota.

I went to a seafood disco the other night and ended up pulling a mussel.

. . . .

I was recently hired to run the Old MacDonald Farm. I'm the C-I-E-I-O.

. . . .

Q: Did you hear about the bored banker?

A: They lost interest in everything.

. . . .

I never buy preshredded cheese because shredding it yourself is grate.

Q: What do scholars eat
when they're hungry?

A: Academia nuts.

. . . .

To the person who invented
zero: Thanks for nothing.

. . . .

Q: What's blue and doesn't weigh very much?

A: Light blue.

. . . .

My son was determined to climb the stairs,
so I wrote him a step-by-step guide.

A dad submitted 10 different puns to a joke contest sponsored by a local newspaper. He hoped that at least one would make the final round. Unfortunately, no pun in 10 did.

. . . .

I don't play soccer because I want to go pro—I'm just doing it for kicks!

. . . .

Q: Which US state has the most streets?

A: Rhode Island.

. . . .

Q: What do you get from a pampered cow?

A: Spoiled milk.

My wife and I let astrology get
between us. It Taurus apart.

. . . .

Q: What do you call a coupon-using vampire?

A: A sucker for good deals!

. . . .

Q: Why are bakers so rich?

A: They make a lot of dough.

. . . .

A pair of cows were talking in the field. One
says, "Have you heard about the mad cow
disease that's going around?" "Yeah," the other
cow says. "Makes me glad I'm a penguin."

Q: Why does Waldo wear a striped shirt?

A: Because he doesn't want to be spotted.

. . . .

Q: Did you hear about the cheese
that's been working out?

A: The dude is shredded.

. . . .

My boss asked me why I only get
sick on weekdays. I said it must be
my weekend immune system.

. . . .

Q: Why does Sherlock Holmes
love Mexican restaurants?

A: They give him good case ideas.

Q: What do you call a zombie while he's cooking stir-fry?

A: Dead man wok-ing.

. . . .

I asked the librarian where they keep the books about paranoia. She looked up and whispered, "They're right behind you."

. . . .

Q: What did the shy pebble wish for?

A: To be a little boulder.

. . . .

Q: Did you hear about the guy who got kicked out of the secret cooking society?

A: He spilled the beans.

The hiring manager asked me if I could perform under pressure. I said I wasn't too familiar with that one, but I could whistle a mean version of "Bohemian Rhapsody."

. . . .

Q: What do you call two octopuses that look the same?

A: I-tentacle.

. . . .

I saw a thousand-year-old oil stain.
It was from ancient Greece.

. . . .

Q: How do you tell the difference between an alligator and a crocodile?

A: You will see one later and one in a while.

I was in a grocery store when a man
started to throw cheese, butter,
and yogurt at me. How dairy!

· · · · · · · · · · · ·

Q: Where does the cake rise?

A: In the yeast.

· · · · · · · · · · · ·

When my partner is sad, I let her color in my
tattoos. She just wants a shoulder to crayon.

· · · · · · · · · · · ·

Q: What's a complementary
snack to ladyfingers?

A: Mentos.

Q: What do you call Batman
when he's injured?

A: Bruised Wayne.

· · · · · · · · · · · ·

I told my wife that a husband is like a fine
wine: he just gets better with age. The
next day she locked me in the cellar.

· · · · · · · · · · · ·

Q: How can you tell it's a dogwood tree?

A: By the bark.

· · · · · · · · · · · ·

Two Wi-Fi engineers got married.
The reception was fantastic.

Q: What kind of music do planets like?

A: Neptunes.

. . . .

Four fonts walk into a bar. The bartender says, "Sorry, we don't serve your type here."

. . . .

Q: What's red and bad for your teeth?

A: A brick!

. . . .

I bought the world's worst thesaurus yesterday. Not only is it terrible; it's terrible.

Q: What did Mario say when he broke up with Princess Peach?

A: "It's not you; it's-a me, Mario!"

· · · · · · · · · · ·

I have the attention of a goldfish. Seriously, it's been watching me for hours.

· · · · · · · · · · ·

Q: What's a calendar's favorite treat?

A: Dates!

· · · · · · · · · · ·

The government announced plans to ban the fifth month of the year. Everyone was dismayed.

Q: What do you call a shoe
made from a banana?

A: A slipper.

. . . .

Within minutes, the detectives identified
the murder weapon. It was a brief case.

. . . .

I took my dog to a pond in a park.
Unfortunately, the ducks kept trying
to bite him. That's what I get for
buying a pure-bread dog.

. . . .

I know some jokes about retired
people, but none of them work.

Q: Why did the farmer try a career in music?

A: He had a ton of sick beets.

. . . .

I think my wife is putting glue on my antique weapons collection. She denies it, but I'm sticking to my guns.

. . . .

Q: How does a cereal pay its bills?

A: With Chex.

. . . .

Q: What's a lawyer's favorite drink?

A: Subpoena colada.

Never date a tennis player. Love means nothing to them.

. . . .

I had a dream that I weighed less than a thousandth of a gram. I was like, 0mg.

. . . .

Q: Why are nurses constantly running out of red crayons?

A: Because they're always drawing blood.

. . . .

A panic-stricken man explained to his doctor, "You have to help me! I think I'm shrinking." "Now settle down," the doctor calmly told him. "You'll just have to learn to be a little patient."

Q: What do you call an illegally parked frog?

A: Toad.

. . . .

I just got fired from my job as a set designer. I left without making a scene.

. . . .

Q: When did they find water on the moon?

A: When it was waning!

. . . .

To the person who stole my bed:
I won't rest until I find you.

Q: What did the drummer
call his twin daughters?

A: Anna One, Anna Two.

. . . .

One of the cows didn't produce milk
today. It was an udder failure.

. . . .

I used to be addicted to soap,
but I'm clean now.

. . . .

KID: Dad, how do I look?

DAD: With your eyes.

The rotation of the earth really makes my day.

. . . .

Someone complimented my parking today. They left a sweet note on the windshield that said, "Parking fine."

. . . .

Q: Did you hear the rumor about the butter?

A: Well, I'm not going to spread it.

. . . .

Q: How do you deal with a fear of speed bumps?

A: You slowly get over it.

It's easy to convince moms not to eat Tide Pods, but it's harder to deter gents.

. . . .

Q: How does a salad say grace?

A: "Lettuce pray."

. . . .

Q: Did you hear about the stolen cheddar?

A: A classic case of nacho cheese.

. . . .

I sat next to a baby on a 10-hour flight. I didn't think it was possible for someone to cry for 10 hours straight. Even the baby was impressed I pulled it off.

Shout-out to my fingers. I can
always count on them.

. . . .

I was once addicted to the Hokey Pokey,
but I was able to turn myself around.

. . . .

Do I enjoy making courthouse puns? Guilty.

. . . .

Q: What country's capital is
growing the fastest?

A: Ireland. Every day it's Dublin.

Bad puns are how eye roll.

. . . .

Q: What's the leading cause of dry skin?
A: Towels.

. . . .

Lately, people have been making apocalypse
jokes like there's no tomorrow.

. . . .

Poop jokes aren't my favorite jokes,
but they're a solid number two.

. . . .

Q: How did the hipster burn his tongue?
A: He ate his food before it was cool.

A turtle is crossing the road when he's mugged by two snails. When the police ask him what happened, the shaken turtle replies, "I don't know. It all happened so fast."

. . . .

My least favorite color is purple. I like it less than red and blue combined.

. . . .

After 65 years of marriage, my grandpa still calls my grandma "honey," "sweetie," "baby," and "sugar." I asked him for the secret to keeping love alive so long. He said, "I forgot her name 10 years ago, and I'm too afraid to ask."

Q: Do you know the last thing my grandfather said to me before he kicked the bucket?

A: "Grandson, watch how far I can kick this bucket."

. . . .

I got a hen to count her own eggs.
She's a real mathemachicken!

. . . .

Q: Did you hear about the scarecrow award?

A: Outstanding in its field.

. . . .

Q: What's the best time to go to the dentist?

A: Tooth hurt-y.

I ordered a chicken and an egg online. I'll let you know.

. . . .

Q: Did you hear about the guy who ironed his four-leaf clover?

A: Really pressed his luck.

. . . .

Milk is the fastest liquid in the world. It's pasteurized before you can see it.

. . . .

Q: How many famous people were born on your birthday?

A: None—only babies.

Q: What do you call a fake noodle?

A: An impasta.

· · · · · · · · · · ·

The other day I started a conversation with a dolphin. We just clicked.

· · · · · · · · · · ·

Q: What is a speech therapist's favorite brand of shoes?

A: Converse.

· · · · · · · · · · ·

The best nap time of the day is 6:30, hands down.

Q: Dad, can you help me out?

A: Sure. Which way did you come in?

. . . .

Q: Did you hear about the kidnapping at school?

A: It's OK, he woke up.

. . . .

A good elevator joke works on so many levels.

. . . .

Q: Have you ever tried to eat a clock?

A: It's very time-consuming.

Q: Which friends are the best kind to eat with?

A: Your taste buds.

. . . .

My friend keeps saying, "Cheer up, man. It could be worse—you could be stuck underground in a hole full of water." I know he means well.

. . . .

Q: Did you hear the World Champion Tongue Twister was arrested the other day?

A: They're going to give him a tough sentence.

. . . .

Q: Why do melons have weddings?

A: Because they cantaloupe!

The wedding was so beautiful,
even the cake was in tiers.

. . . .

Q: What's the difference between
ignorance and indifference?

A: I don't know, and I don't care.

. . . .

Want to hear a joke about paper?
Never mind . . . it's tearable.

. . . .

Q: Why did the cops arrest the chicken?

A: They suspected fowl play.

I told a coworker that I thought
they drew their eyebrows in too
high. They seemed surprised.

. . . .

Q: Where does light go when it's been bad?

A: To prism.

. . . .

I think I might have bad posture,
but it's just a hunch.

. . . .

I once skipped school to go bungee jumping
with friends. We all got suspended.

Q: What do prisoners use to call each other?

A: Their cell phones.

. . . .

I hung a framed copy of the
US Constitution on my wall. It is
a decoration of independence.

. . . .

Q: Did you know the first french
fries weren't cooked in France?

A: They were cooked in Greece.

. . . .

I was about to get carded at the liquor store,
and my Blockbuster card accidentally fell out
of my wallet. The cashier said, "Never mind."

Q: Why are skeletons so calm?

A: Nothing gets under their skin.

. . . .

I want to organize a hide-and-seek league,
but good players are hard to find.

. . . .

Q: Where can you find the most
superheroes in one place?

A: Cape Town.

. . . .

I slept like a log last night.
Woke up in the fireplace!

Not to brag, but I made seven figures last year. Turns out I was the worst employee at the toy factory.

. . . .

Q: What do you call a Frenchman wearing sandals?

A: Philippe Flop.

. . . .

There are two muffins baking in the oven. One muffin says to the other, "Phew, is it getting hot in here, or is it just me?" The other muffin says, "AAAAHHH! A TALKING MUFFIN!"

. . . .

Q: What's an astronaut's favorite part of a computer?

A: The space bar.

Q: Why can't you hear a pterodactyl using the bathroom?

A: Because the *P* is silent.

. . . .

If you see a crime at an Apple Store, does that make you an iWitness?

. . . .

SON: Dad, did you get a haircut?

DAD: No, I got them all cut!

. . . .

Q: How do you get a squirrel to like you?

A: You act like a nut.

This graveyard looks overcrowded.
People must be dying to get in.

. . . .

Q: Why can't you send a duck to space?

A: Because the bill would be astronomical.

. . . .

Q: What do you call Bill Gates
when he's flying?

A: A Bill-in-air.

. . . .

I'm really excited for the amateur autopsy club
I just joined. Tuesday is open Mike night!

I have an inferiority complex, but it's not a very good one.

. . . .

Q: Did you know that bees are allergic to pollen?

A: They break out in hives.

. . . .

I rubbed ketchup in my eyes to see more clearly. You know what they say: Heinzsight is 20/20.

. . . .

I finally started watching that documentary on clocks. It was about time.

The first time I got a universal remote control,
I thought, "This changes everything."

. . . .

Q: How does a hog sign its name?

A: With a pig pen.

. . . .

So what if I don't know the definition of
apocalypse? It's not the end of the world.

. . . .

Q: Why is the letter *A* like a flower?

A: Because a *B* always comes after it!

A book fell on my head the other day.
I have only my shelf to blame.

. . . .

A teacher orders his fifth coffee for the day.
"I'm so frustrated," he complains to the
barista. "Our school system is incredibly
disorganized, and nothing works as it should."
"Well, then, I guess it's true," the barista
says. "School prepares you for real life."

. . . .

The guy who stole my diary died yesterday,
so my thoughts are with his family.

. . . .

Don't spell *part* backward. It's a trap.

Q: What's a horse's top priority when voting?

A: A stable economy!

· · · · · · · · · · ·

I can tolerate math, maybe even
a little algebra, but geometry
is where I draw the line.

· · · · · · · · · · ·

Q: What would the Terminator be
called after his retirement?

A: The Exterminator.

· · · · · · · · · · ·

I put my grandma on speed
dial. I call that Instagram.

My son knocked a picture of himself off the shelf. He looked devastated. I told him, "Don't worry about it, kiddo. Pick yourself up."

. . . .

Q: How did the barber win the race?

A: He knew a shortcut.

. . . .

My new sweater had a problem with static, so I returned it. They gave me a new one free of charge.

. . . .

Q: Why did the orange lose the race?

A: It ran out of juice.

ME: I lost an electron.

FRIEND: Are you sure?

ME: Yep, I'm positive.

. . . .

A man visited a film studio and was browsing the wardrobe archives. He asked a costume designer which were her favorite pieces. She replied, "Well, that shirt there was worn by Pacino. That jacket was put together for De Niro. And these boots were made for Walken."

. . . .

Q: Why did the golfer wear two pairs of pants?

A: In case he got a hole in one!

I accidentally handed my daughter
the glue stick instead of the ChapStick.
She still isn't speaking to me.

. . . .

Q: What do you call a person
in a tree with a briefcase?

A: A branch manager.

. . . .

Where there is a will, there is a relative.

. . . .

It's hard to explain puns to kleptomaniacs.
They are always taking things literally.

I got an email the other day teaching
me how to read maps backward.
Turns out it was just spam.

．．．．．．．．．．．

My friend's gambling habit is getting out
of hand. The other day he tried to bet his
newborn son in our game of poker, and
I thought I might have to raise him.

．．．．．．．．．．．

Q: Did you hear about the guy
who invented Life Savers?

A: They say he made a mint!

．．．．．．．．．．．

There are three kinds of people: those
who can count and those who can't.

Q: What does the sourdough dad do at night?

A: Tells breadtime stories.

. . . .

After dinner, my dad asked if I could clear the table. I needed a running start, but I made it!

. . . .

To keep the dream alive, it's best
to hit the snooze button.

. . . .

I asked my friend to meet me at the gym,
but he never showed up. I guess the
two of us aren't going to work out.

For a while, Houdini would use a trap door in every one of his shows. I guess you could say he was going through a stage.

. . . .

Q: What do you call a fish with no eye?

A: A fsh.

. . . .

When everything is coming your way, you're in the wrong lane.

. . . .

I know 25 letters of the alphabet. I don't know Y.

Q: Did you hear about the square
that got into a bike accident?

A: Yeah, now he's a rect-angle!

. . . .

Justice is a dish best served cold. If it were
served warm, it would be justwater.

. . . .

My friend is obsessed with monorails.
He really has a one-track mind.

. . . .

Q: What did the photon say
to the hotel bellhop?

A: "No luggage; I'm traveling light."

If a pig loses its voice, does that
mean it's disgruntled?

· · · · · · · · · · ·

Q: What does a nosy pepper do?

A: It gets jalapeño business!

· · · · · · · · · · ·

Q: What do you call a bear with no teeth?

A: A gummy bear!

· · · · · · · · · · ·

I wouldn't buy anything with
Velcro. It's a total rip-off.

I went to the zoo and saw a
baguette in a cage. The zookeeper
said it was bread in captivity.

• • • • • • • • • • •

Q: Why was the belt sent to jail?

A: For holding up a pair of pants!

• • • • • • • • • • •

I paused and then said to my kid, "You aren't
even listening, are you?" My kid replied, "That's
a pretty weird way to start a conversation."

• • • • • • • • • • •

DAUGHTER: Dad, can I watch the TV?

DAD: Sure, just don't turn it on.

A woman was shopping at the grocery store in preparation for Thanksgiving dinner. As she looked at the large selection of frozen turkeys, she was disappointed that none of them were big enough for the gathering she had planned. She found the butcher and asked, "Do these turkeys get any bigger?" "No ma'am," the butcher said. "They're dead."

. . . .

Geology rocks, but geography is where it's at.

. . . .

Q: Why did the computer
get mad at the printer?

A: Because it didn't like its toner.

A friend asked,
"Why don't you stop
writing just a bunch of
jokes and start writing
an actual book?" I replied,
"That's a novel idea."

ABOUT THE AUTHOR

Slade Wentworth is a writer and creative entrepre-
neur who'd rather be cooking with his kids. You
can follow his dad humor and family recipes on
Instagram and TikTok **@THEDADBRIEFS**.